Essential Ir

My D

Name

Address

Contact Number

Email

Passport Number

Country of issue

Medical info

Emergency Contact

Name

Relationship

Address

Contact Number

Email

Insurance Info

Provider

Policy Number

Contact Number

Embassy Info

Where next?

Depart	Return	Location

My Trip To _____

Departure Date	_____	Return Date	
Flight No		Flight No	
Airport		Airport	
Departure Time		Departure Time	
Arrival Time		Arrival Time	
Transport to Airport	_____	Transport to Airport	_____
Transport to Accommodation	_____	Transport to Home	_____
Accommodation	_____		

Things to pack

☐
☐
☐
☐
☐
☐
☐
☐
☐
☐
☐
☐
☐
☐
☐

☐
☐
☐
☐
☐
☐
☐
☐
☐
☐
☐
☐
☐
☐
☐

Trip Itinerary

Date	Time	Activity/Event

Trip Planning

Places to try eating at

Places to see

Activities to try

Transport information

Notes

My Trip To _____

Departure Date _____   Return Date _____

Flight No		Flight No	
Airport		Airport	
Departure Time		Departure Time	
Arrival Time		Arrival Time	
Transport to Airport		Transport to Airport	
Transport to Accommodation		Transport to Home	
Accommodation			

Things to pack

	☐		☐
	☐		☐
	☐		☐
	☐		☐
	☐		☐
	☐		☐
	☐		☐
	☐		☐
	☐		☐
	☐		☐
	☐		☐
	☐		☐
	☐		☐
	☐		☐

Trip Itinerary

Date	Time	Activity/Event

Trip Planning

Places to try eating at

Places to see

Activities to try

Transport information

Notes

My Trip To _____

Departure Date _____ Return Date _____

Flight No		Flight No	
Airport		Airport	
Departure Time		Departure Time	
Arrival Time		Arrival Time	
Transport to Airport		Transport to Airport	
Transport to Accommodation		Transport to Home	

Accommodation _____

Things to pack

	☐		☐
_____	☐	_____	☐
_____	☐	_____	☐
_____	☐	_____	☐
_____	☐	_____	☐
_____	☐	_____	☐
_____	☐	_____	☐
_____	☐	_____	☐
_____	☐	_____	☐
_____	☐	_____	☐
_____	☐	_____	☐
_____	☐	_____	☐
_____	☐	_____	☐
_____	☐	_____	☐
_____	☐	_____	☐

Trip Itinerary

Date	Time	Activity/Event

Trip Planning

Places to try eating at

Places to see

Activities to try

Transport information

Notes

My Trip To _____

Departure Date		Return Date	
Flight No		Flight No	
Airport		Airport	
Departure Time		Departure Time	
Arrival Time		Arrival Time	
Transport to Airport		Transport to Airport	
Transport to Accommodation		Transport to Home	
Accommodation			

Things to pack

	☐		☐
	☐		☐
	☐		☐
	☐		☐
	☐		☐
	☐		☐
	☐		☐
	☐		☐
	☐		☐
	☐		☐
	☐		☐
	☐		☐
	☐		☐
	☐		☐
	☐		☐

Trip Itinerary

Date	Time	Activity/Event

Trip Planning

Places to try eating at

_____

_____

_____

_____

_____

Places to see

_____

_____

_____

_____

Activities to try

_____

_____

_____

_____

Transport information

_____

_____

_____

_____

_____

_____

Notes

My Trip To _____

| Departure Date | _____ | Return Date | _____ |

Flight No		Flight No	
Airport		Airport	
Departure Time		Departure Time	
Arrival Time		Arrival Time	
Transport to Airport		Transport to Airport	
Transport to Accommodation		Transport to Home	
Accommodation			

Things to pack

	☐		☐
_____	☐	_____	☐
_____	☐	_____	☐
_____	☐	_____	☐
_____	☐	_____	☐
_____	☐	_____	☐
_____	☐	_____	☐
_____	☐	_____	☐
_____	☐	_____	☐
_____	☐	_____	☐
_____	☐	_____	☐
_____	☐	_____	☐
_____	☐	_____	☐
_____	☐	_____	☐
_____	☐	_____	☐
_____	☐	_____	☐

Trip Itinerary

Date	Time	Activity/Event

Trip Planning

Places to try eating at

_____

_____

_____

_____

_____

_____

Places to see

_____

_____

_____

_____

_____

Activities to try

_____

_____

_____

_____

_____

Transport information

_____

_____

_____

_____

_____

_____

_____

Notes

My Trip To _____

Departure Date		Return Date	
Flight No		Flight No	
Airport		Airport	
Departure Time		Departure Time	
Arrival Time		Arrival Time	
Transport to Airport		Transport to Airport	
Transport to Accommodation		Transport to Home	
Accommodation			

Things to pack

	☐		☐
	☐		☐
	☐		☐
	☐		☐
	☐		☐
	☐		☐
	☐		☐
	☐		☐
	☐		☐
	☐		☐
	☐		☐
	☐		☐
	☐		☐
	☐		☐
	☐		☐

Trip Itinerary

Date	Time	Activity/Event

Trip Planning

Places to try eating at

Places to see

Activities to try

Transport information

Notes

My Trip To _____

Departure Date	_____	Return Date	
Flight No		Flight No	
Airport		Airport	
Departure Time		Departure Time	
Arrival Time		Arrival Time	
Transport to Airport	_____	Transport to Airport	_____
Transport to Accommodation	_____	Transport to Home	_____
Accommodation	_____		

Things to pack

_____	☐	_____	☐
_____	☐	_____	☐
_____	☐	_____	☐
_____	☐	_____	☐
_____	☐	_____	☐
_____	☐	_____	☐
_____	☐	_____	☐
_____	☐	_____	☐
_____	☐	_____	☐
_____	☐	_____	☐
_____	☐	_____	☐
_____	☐	_____	☐
_____	☐	_____	☐
_____	☐	_____	☐
	☐		☐

Trip Itinerary

Date	Time	Activity/Event

Trip Planning

Places to try eating at

Places to see

Activities to try

Transport information

Notes

My Trip To _____

Departure Date		Return Date	
Flight No		Flight No	
Airport		Airport	
Departure Time		Departure Time	
Arrival Time		Arrival Time	
Transport to Airport		Transport to Airport	
Transport to Accommodation		Transport to Home	
Accommodation			

Things to pack

☐
☐
☐
☐
☐
☐
☐
☐
☐
☐
☐
☐
☐
☐
☐

☐
☐
☐
☐
☐
☐
☐
☐
☐
☐
☐
☐
☐
☐
☐

Trip Itinerary

Date	Time	Activity/Event

Trip Planning

Places to try eating at

Places to see

Activities to try

Transport information

Notes

My Trip To _____

Departure Date	_____	Return Date	_____
Flight No		Flight No	
Airport		Airport	
Departure Time		Departure Time	
Arrival Time		Arrival Time	
Transport to Airport		Transport to Airport	
Transport to Accommodation		Transport to Home	
Accommodation			

Things to pack

	☐		☐
	☐		☐
	☐		☐
	☐		☐
	☐		☐
	☐		☐
	☐		☐
	☐		☐
	☐		☐
	☐		☐
	☐		☐
	☐		☐
	☐		☐
	☐		☐
	☐		☐

Trip Itinerary

Date	Time	Activity/Event

Trip Planning

Places to try eating at

Places to see

Activities to try

Transport information

Notes

My Trip To _____

| Departure Date | ———— | Return Date | ———— |

Flight No		Flight No	
Airport		Airport	
Departure Time		Departure Time	
Arrival Time		Arrival Time	
Transport to	————	Transport to	————
Airport	————	Airport	————
Transport to	————	Transport to	————
Accommodation		Home	

Accommodation ————————————————————

Things to pack

	☐		☐
————	☐	————	☐
————	☐	————	☐
————	☐	————	☐
————	☐	————	☐
————	☐	————	☐
————	☐	————	☐
————	☐	————	☐
————	☐	————	☐
————	☐	————	☐
————	☐	————	☐
————	☐	————	☐
————	☐	————	☐
————	☐	————	☐
————	☐	————	☐

Trip Itinerary

Date	Time	Activity/Event

Trip Planning

Places to try eating at

Places to see

Activities to try

Transport information

Notes

My Trip To _____

Departure Date _____   Return Date _____

Flight No		Flight No	
Airport		Airport	
Departure Time		Departure Time	
Arrival Time		Arrival Time	
Transport to Airport		Transport to Airport	
Transport to Accommodation		Transport to Home	

Accommodation _____

Things to pack

	☐		☐
	☐		☐
	☐		☐
	☐		☐
	☐		☐
	☐		☐
	☐		☐
	☐		☐
	☐		☐
	☐		☐
	☐		☐
	☐		☐
	☐		☐
	☐		☐
	☐		☐

Trip Itinerary

Date	Time	Activity/Event

Trip Planning

Places to try eating at

Places to see

Activities to try

Transport information

Notes

My Trip To _____

Departure Date	_____	Return Date	_____

Flight No		Flight No	
Airport		Airport	
Departure Time		Departure Time	
Arrival Time		Arrival Time	
Transport to Airport	_____	Transport to Airport	_____
Transport to Accommodation	_____	Transport to Home	_____

Accommodation _____

Things to pack

_____	☐	☐
_____	☐	☐
_____	☐	☐
_____	☐	☐
_____	☐	☐
_____	☐	☐
_____	☐	☐
_____	☐	☐
_____	☐	☐
_____	☐	☐
_____	☐	☐
_____	☐	☐
_____	☐	☐
_____	☐	☐
_____	☐	☐

Trip Itinerary

Date	Time	Activity/Event

Trip Planning

Places to try eating at

Places to see

Activities to try

Transport information

Notes

My Trip To _____

Departure Date _____   Return Date _____

Flight No		Flight No	
Airport		Airport	
Departure Time		Departure Time	
Arrival Time		Arrival Time	
Transport to Airport		Transport to Airport	
Transport to Accommodation		Transport to Home	
Accommodation			

Things to pack

	☐		☐
	☐		☐
	☐		☐
	☐		☐
	☐		☐
	☐		☐
	☐		☐
	☐		☐
	☐		☐
	☐		☐
	☐		☐
	☐		☐
	☐		☐
	☐		☐
	☐		☐
	☐		☐

Trip Itinerary

Date	Time	Activity/Event

Trip Planning

Places to try eating at

_____

_____

_____

_____

_____

Places to see

_____

_____

_____

_____

Activities to try

_____

_____

_____

_____

Transport information

_____

_____

_____

_____

_____

Notes

My Trip To _____

Departure Date		Return Date	
Flight No		Flight No	
Airport		Airport	
Departure Time		Departure Time	
Arrival Time		Arrival Time	
Transport to Airport		Transport to Airport	
Transport to Accommodation		Transport to Home	
Accommodation			

Things to pack

- ☐
- ☐
- ☐
- ☐
- ☐
- ☐
- ☐
- ☐
- ☐
- ☐
- ☐
- ☐
- ☐
- ☐
- ☐

- ☐
- ☐
- ☐
- ☐
- ☐
- ☐
- ☐
- ☐
- ☐
- ☐
- ☐
- ☐
- ☐
- ☐
- ☐

Trip Itinerary

Date	Time	Activity/Event

Trip Planning

Places to try eating at

Places to see

Activities to try

Transport information

Notes

My Trip To _____

Departure Date	_____		Return Date	_____

Flight No		Flight No	
Airport		Airport	
Departure Time		Departure Time	
Arrival Time		Arrival Time	
Transport to Airport	_____	Transport to Airport	_____
Transport to Accommodation	_____	Transport to Home	_____
Accommodation	_____		

Things to pack

_____	☐	_____	☐
_____	☐	_____	☐
_____	☐	_____	☐
_____	☐	_____	☐
_____	☐	_____	☐
_____	☐	_____	☐
_____	☐	_____	☐
_____	☐	_____	☐
_____	☐	_____	☐
_____	☐	_____	☐
_____	☐	_____	☐
_____	☐	_____	☐
_____	☐	_____	☐
_____	☐	_____	☐
_____	☐	_____	☐
_____	☐	_____	☐

Trip Itinerary

Date	Time	Activity/Event

Trip Planning

Places to try eating at

_____

_____

_____

_____

_____

_____

Places to see

_____

_____

_____

_____

_____

Activities to try

_____

_____

_____

_____

Transport information

_____

_____

_____

_____

_____

_____

Notes

My Trip To _____

Departure Date		Return Date	
Flight No		Flight No	
Airport		Airport	
Departure Time		Departure Time	
Arrival Time		Arrival Time	
Transport to Airport		Transport to Airport	
Transport to Accommodation		Transport to Home	
Accommodation			

Things to pack

- ☐
- ☐
- ☐
- ☐
- ☐
- ☐
- ☐
- ☐
- ☐
- ☐
- ☐
- ☐
- ☐
- ☐

- ☐
- ☐
- ☐
- ☐
- ☐
- ☐
- ☐
- ☐
- ☐
- ☐
- ☐
- ☐
- ☐
- ☐

Trip Itinerary

Date	Time	Activity/Event

Trip Planning

Places to try eating at

Places to see

Activities to try

Transport information

Notes

My Trip To _____

Departure Date	_____	Return Date	_____
Flight No		Flight No	
Airport		Airport	
Departure Time		Departure Time	
Arrival Time		Arrival Time	
Transport to Airport	_____	Transport to Airport	_____
Transport to Accommodation	_____	Transport to Home	_____

Accommodation _____

Things to pack

	☐		☐
_____	☐	_____	☐
_____	☐	_____	☐
_____	☐	_____	☐
_____	☐	_____	☐
_____	☐	_____	☐
_____	☐	_____	☐
_____	☐	_____	☐
_____	☐	_____	☐
_____	☐	_____	☐
_____	☐	_____	☐
_____	☐	_____	☐
_____	☐	_____	☐
_____	☐	_____	☐
_____	☐	_____	☐

Trip Itinerary

Date	Time	Activity/Event

Trip Planning

Places to try eating at

Places to see

Activities to try

Transport information

Notes

My Trip To _____

Departure Date		Return Date	
Flight No		Flight No	
Airport		Airport	
Departure Time		Departure Time	
Arrival Time		Arrival Time	
Transport to Airport		Transport to Airport	
Transport to Accommodation		Transport to Home	
Accommodation			

Things to pack

	☐		☐
	☐		☐
	☐		☐
	☐		☐
	☐		☐
	☐		☐
	☐		☐
	☐		☐
	☐		☐
	☐		☐
	☐		☐
	☐		☐
	☐		☐
	☐		☐

Trip Itinerary

Date	Time	Activity/Event

Trip Planning

Places to try eating at

Places to see

Activities to try

Transport information

Notes

My Trip To _____

Departure Date		Return Date	
Flight No		Flight No	
Airport		Airport	
Departure Time		Departure Time	
Arrival Time		Arrival Time	
Transport to Airport		Transport to Airport	
Transport to Accommodation		Transport to Home	
Accommodation			

Things to pack

	☐		☐
	☐		☐
	☐		☐
	☐		☐
	☐		☐
	☐		☐
	☐		☐
	☐		☐
	☐		☐
	☐		☐
	☐		☐
	☐		☐
	☐		☐
	☐		☐
	☐		☐

Trip Itinerary

Date	Time	Activity/Event

Trip Planning

Places to try eating at

Places to see

Activities to try

Transport information

Notes

My Trip To _____

Departure Date _____   Return Date _____

Flight No		Flight No	
Airport		Airport	
Departure Time		Departure Time	
Arrival Time		Arrival Time	
Transport to Airport		Transport to Airport	
Transport to Accommodation		Transport to Home	
Accommodation			

Things to pack

	☐		☐
	☐		☐
	☐		☐
	☐		☐
	☐		☐
	☐		☐
	☐		☐
	☐		☐
	☐		☐
	☐		☐
	☐		☐
	☐		☐
	☐		☐
	☐		☐
	☐		☐

Trip Itinerary

Date	Time	Activity/Event

Trip Planning

Places to try eating at

Places to see

Activities to try

Transport information

Notes

My Trip To _____

Departure Date		Return Date	
Flight No		Flight No	
Airport		Airport	
Departure Time		Departure Time	
Arrival Time		Arrival Time	
Transport to Airport		Transport to Airport	
Transport to Accommodation		Transport to Home	
Accommodation			

Things to pack

☐
☐
☐
☐
☐
☐
☐
☐
☐
☐
☐
☐
☐
☐

Trip Itinerary

Date	Time	Activity/Event

Trip Planning

Places to try eating at

Places to see

Activities to try

Transport information

Notes

My Trip To _____

Departure Date		Return Date	
Flight No		Flight No	
Airport		Airport	
Departure Time		Departure Time	
Arrival Time		Arrival Time	
Transport to Airport		Transport to Airport	
Transport to Accommodation		Transport to Home	
Accommodation			

Things to pack

	☐		☐
	☐		☐
	☐		☐
	☐		☐
	☐		☐
	☐		☐
	☐		☐
	☐		☐
	☐		☐
	☐		☐
	☐		☐
	☐		☐
	☐		☐
	☐		☐
	☐		☐
	☐		☐

Trip Itinerary

Date	Time	Activity/Event

Trip Planning

Places to try eating at

Places to see

Activities to try

Transport information

Notes

My Trip To _____

Departure Date		Return Date	
Flight No		Flight No	
Airport		Airport	
Departure Time		Departure Time	
Arrival Time		Arrival Time	
Transport to Airport		Transport to Airport	
Transport to Accommodation		Transport to Home	
Accommodation			

Things to pack

	☐		☐
	☐		☐
	☐		☐
	☐		☐
	☐		☐
	☐		☐
	☐		☐
	☐		☐
	☐		☐
	☐		☐
	☐		☐
	☐		☐
	☐		☐
	☐		☐

Trip Itinerary

Date	Time	Activity/Event

Trip Planning

Places to try eating at

Places to see

Activities to try

Transport information

Notes

My Trip To _____

Departure Date		Return Date	
Flight No		Flight No	
Airport		Airport	
Departure Time		Departure Time	
Arrival Time		Arrival Time	
Transport to Airport		Transport to Airport	
Transport to Accommodation		Transport to Home	
Accommodation			

Things to pack

	☐		☐
	☐		☐
	☐		☐
	☐		☐
	☐		☐
	☐		☐
	☐		☐
	☐		☐
	☐		☐
	☐		☐
	☐		☐
	☐		☐
	☐		☐
	☐		☐

Trip Itinerary

Date	Time	Activity/Event

Trip Planning

Places to try eating at

Places to see

Activities to try

Transport information

Notes

My Trip To _____

Departure Date		**Return Date**	
Flight No		Flight No	
Airport		Airport	
Departure Time		Departure Time	
Arrival Time		Arrival Time	
Transport to Airport		Transport to Airport	
Transport to Accommodation		Transport to Home	
Accommodation			

Things to pack

	☐		☐
	☐		☐
	☐		☐
	☐		☐
	☐		☐
	☐		☐
	☐		☐
	☐		☐
	☐		☐
	☐		☐
	☐		☐
	☐		☐
	☐		☐
	☐		☐
	☐		☐

Trip Itinerary

Date	Time	Activity/Event

Trip Planning

Places to try eating at

_____

_____

_____

_____

_____

_____

Places to see

_____

_____

_____

_____

_____

Activities to try

_____

_____

_____

_____

_____

Transport information

_____

_____

_____

_____

_____

_____

Notes

My Trip To _____

Departure Date _____   Return Date _____

Flight No		Flight No	
Airport		Airport	
Departure Time		Departure Time	
Arrival Time		Arrival Time	
Transport to Airport		Transport to Airport	
Transport to Accommodation		Transport to Home	

Accommodation _____

Things to pack

☐
☐
☐
☐
☐
☐
☐
☐
☐
☐
☐
☐
☐
☐
☐
☐

☐
☐
☐
☐
☐
☐
☐
☐
☐
☐
☐
☐
☐
☐
☐
☐

Trip Itinerary

Date	Time	Activity/Event

Trip Planning

Places to try eating at

Places to see

Activities to try

Transport information

Notes

My Trip To _____

Departure Date	_____	Return Date	_____
Flight No		Flight No	
Airport		Airport	
Departure Time		Departure Time	
Arrival Time		Arrival Time	
Transport to Airport		Transport to Airport	
Transport to Accommodation		Transport to Home	
Accommodation			

Things to pack

	☐		☐
	☐		☐
	☐		☐
	☐		☐
	☐		☐
	☐		☐
	☐		☐
	☐		☐
	☐		☐
	☐		☐
	☐		☐
	☐		☐
	☐		☐
	☐		☐

Trip Itinerary

Date	Time	Activity/Event

Trip Planning

Places to try eating at

_____

_____

_____

_____

_____

Places to see

_____

_____

_____

_____

Activities to try

_____

_____

_____

_____

Transport information

_____

_____

_____

_____

_____

_____

Notes

My Trip To _____

Departure Date _____   Return Date _____

Flight No		Flight No	
Airport		Airport	
Departure Time		Departure Time	
Arrival Time		Arrival Time	
Transport to Airport		Transport to Airport	
Transport to Accommodation		Transport to Home	
Accommodation			

Things to pack

	☐		☐
	☐		☐
	☐		☐
	☐		☐
	☐		☐
	☐		☐
	☐		☐
	☐		☐
	☐		☐
	☐		☐
	☐		☐
	☐		☐
	☐		☐
	☐		☐
	☐		☐

Trip Itinerary

Date	Time	Activity/Event

Trip Planning

Places to try eating at

Places to see

Activities to try

Transport information

Notes

Made in the USA
Monee, IL
12 January 2021